Made for you
AUTUMN

SEASONAL RECIPES FOR GIFTS AND CELEBRATIONS

About Sophie

Born and raised in Sydney, now living with her family on their farm just outside Orange in country New South Wales, Sophie Hansen trained in journalism and has over 20 years' experience as a features writer. She has contributed to *Australian Country Style* and *Outback* magazines; she was an editor for Slow Food International's English website, lived in Italy for 3 years and is fluent in Italian. In 2013 she set up her blog, *Local is Lovely*, and her podcast, *My Open Kitchen*, is going into its third season. Sophie has been awarded Australian Rural Woman of the Year in recognition of her commitment to rural communities. She believes in simple, tasty and seasonal food, made with love and shared generously.

Instagram: @locallovely @myopenkitchen

Made for you
AUTUMN

SEASONAL RECIPES FOR GIFTS AND CELEBRATIONS

Make ~ Wrap ~ Deliver

Sophie Hansen

murdoch books
Sydney | London

CONTENTS

Food for thought

Cooking for others is the best kind of cooking. It's an expression of love, generosity and kindness – and goodness knows we need more and more of that these days. Don't you think?

I hope so! Because this little book you hold, *Made For You: Autumn*, is all about what to cook for your friends and family, exactly when they need it. It's a collection of simple, delicious and easy recipes that your family will love, and that your friends will appreciate beyond words.

From recipes for picnics and small, meaningful gatherings to a chocolate cake recipe that everyone will always love (and love you for), soup, muesli bars, and crumble to fill the hunger gaps of new mothers, recovering patients and hollow-legged teenagers, and recipes for lunches to take to work and perhaps share with your work mates. This is love made edible. This is food that says 'I made this for you because I want you to eat well and feel cared for'.

Autumn is such a wonderful time to be cooking. The generosity of late-harvest bounty means we have figs, tomatoes, plums, berries, apples, quinces and pears to poach, preserve, fold into cake batters, toss through salads and eat straight from the fruit bowl. The recipes in this book celebrate this season and offer a welcome shift from the lightness of summer to the gentle cooler days of autumn and, with them, the baking, braising and more warming dishes we love.

And speaking of figs, it was a tray of figs that inspired the writing of this book. Here's the story; it's about a dear friend of mine, who, a couple of years ago, came home one early autumn afternoon to find a special gift at her door. She'd just finished her last treatment session for breast cancer, and had driven some hours back to her farm, feeling rather queasy, to find a cool box waiting for her. In it was a couple of bottles of ice-cold mineral water, a tray of figs and a chunk of her favourite Gorgonzola cheese. That evening, she sat on the verandah with her partner and toasted the end of her treatment with the mineral water and the cheese and figs. She says it was the best meal of her life, not just because it was so perfect and delicious, but because of the careful thought that had gone into it. Such a simple feast, but so full of love.

I hope this book gives you some new ideas and inspiration to stock up on autumn's best produce and cook up a storm, or rather, some good food to share with the people you love most.

Packing up your care parcels

Here are a few tips for wrapping and packing up your edible care packages so they look as gorgeous as they taste. Keep a stash of pretty tea towels, scraps of fabric and muslin handy – these are great for wrapping up cakes and casseroles. Tie them up with some twine or cute ribbon and tuck a bunch of rosemary or a rose or other flower into the bow. None of this is difficult, but it all adds up to make your edible gifts even more special. Keep an eye out in your local opportunity shops for fabrics, jars and retro casserole dishes (which will probably cost less than disposable foil ones!) and give your beautiful stews, pies and bakes away in these – and it doesn't matter if you never see them again. I have a basket in the pantry where I collect such items, plus a stash of tags and pens so it's easy to wrap up things as they come out of the oven and head out the door.

Add a pretty watercolour gift tag to your basket of home-made goodies.

Practical tips for giving food

Of course, we all need to be careful of food safety when cooking for others, especially when it comes to transporting our edible food gifts. Here are a few rules of thumb to stick to (or you risk doing more harm than good with your well-meaning gifts!).

Wash your hands before cooking and be aware of safe temperatures and storage times. Once cooked, cool food on the bench until the steam stops rising, then place it in the fridge – don't leave food to cool completely on the bench. And don't put hot food straight into the freezer – cool it in the fridge first. Cooked food can generally be safely stored in the fridge for 3 to 4 days only.

To freeze casseroles, divide them into servings of a size that suits your family or the family they are heading to, then place in freezer-safe containers or bags, label with the name of the dish and date, and freeze for 2 to 3 months. Avoid freezer burn by using good thick, resealable bags or quality containers and leave a couple of centimetres at the top of the bag or container to allow the food to expand when frozen. The best and safest place to thaw frozen food is in the fridge.

Watercolour gift tags

My mother, Annie, is an artist and I grew up watching her sketch, paint and doodle all the time. She always encouraged me to do the same and, while I am absolutely no artist myself, I do love creating sweet watercolour tags and labels for jars of jam, wrapped-up loaf cakes and similar. You don't have to paint a masterpiece, just grab a pen and draw an outline and then grab some very forgiving and easy-to-use watercolours to fill them in. Easy! And truly, they look so pretty. Even better if you have kids around – they will love helping out and making up pretty labels of their own.

Beeswax food wraps

These wraps have become popular in recent years as a smart, eco-friendly alternative to plastic wrap. And while you can find them in shops, beeswax wraps are usually fairly expensive. But here's the good news: they're super cheap and easy to make. So grab some fabric (an old shirt or pillowcase) and make up a bunch of wraps to give away as presents and/or wrap gifts, sandwiches for school lunches, cover bowls of leftovers and so on.

You'll need 200 g (7 oz) solid beeswax (find it online or in speciality stores), 1 tablespoon olive oil, pinking shears, an old paintbrush, baking paper, a few baking trays and 6–8 fabric rectangles (they'll need to fit on your baking trays, so use that as a size guide).

Preheat the oven to 150°C (300°F). Line your baking trays with baking paper and place a piece of fabric on each. Melt the beeswax in a glass bowl over a pan of simmering water, stir in the oil, then brush it over the fabric. Pop in the oven for a few minutes, then brush again so the wax evenly and lightly covers the fabric. Hang on a clothesline to dry and they're ready to use. Wash beeswax wraps in lukewarm water, never in the dishwasher! If you find them a bit stiff, just work with your hands for a minute until the warmth makes them pliable.

On our farm, smoko is an early lunch. Or bribery to keep everyone working just a little longer.

Smoko

Apple, fennel and pork sausage rolls ~ Quick tomato chutney
Oatcakes ~ Quince chutney ~ Blackberry and rosemary loaf

Generosity and hospitality are common themes in country cooking. I'm always amazed by the speed with which food is produced in a country kitchen as soon as someone looks hungry. A sandwich, a piece of cake or biscuits appear from nowhere and it seems like the kettle is always on.

I love this easy generosity. I love that because shops are generally a fair drive away, kitchens are well stocked and ready to whip up any manner of sustenance. And I love the tradition of smoko.

Smoko is a substantial snack and rest break in the middle of a morning or afternoon of work. Usually there's something hot to eat and a big pot of tea to share. I have a friend who lives on her family farm west of Broken Hill and every day they make enormous trays of muffins, sausage rolls and quiches for 9am smoko to feed the shearing crews who have been going since 5am.

On our farm, smoko is an early lunch. Or bribery to keep everyone working just a little longer. These sausage rolls with tomato chutney do the trick, and my oatcakes spread with some blue cheese and quince chutney are firm favourites. I also like to sweeten the deal with this moist blackberry loaf.

Quince chutney

APPLE, FENNEL AND PORK SAUSAGE ROLLS

These sausage rolls are excellent for smoko break, lunch or dinner. If serving them as a main meal, add a big salad full of peppery greens and a spicy tomato chutney like the one below. Make up a double batch of sausage rolls and freeze them (uncooked) in long logs, ready to bake from frozen, and you'll be ready to feed the hungry hordes in minutes.

1 Tbsp (20 g) butter
1 tsp fennel seeds
2 granny smith apples, cut into small pieces
1 red onion, diced
500 g (1 lb 2 oz) pork mince
1 Tbsp thyme leaves
3 sheets butter puff pastry, thawed
1 egg, lightly whisked
2 Tbsp sesame seeds
1 tsp sea salt
Quick tomato chutney (see below), to serve

Melt the butter in a heavy-based frying pan over medium–high heat. Add three-quarters of the fennel seeds and the apple pieces and cook for a few minutes or until softened. Reduce the heat to low, add the onion and cook, stirring often, for 10 minutes. Remove from the heat and allow to cool.

Preheat the oven to 200°C (400°F). Line a large baking tray with baking paper.

In a large bowl, mix the pork and thyme with the cooled apple mixture, and season with salt and pepper. Take a third of this mixture and place it on one of the thawed pastry sheets, making a sausage shape along the bottom third of the sheet. Roll as tightly as you can to create one long sausage. Repeat with the remaining pastry and pork mixture.

If you're freezing the sausage rolls at this point, wrap them in plastic wrap and pop them in the freezer. Otherwise, onwards! Using a pastry brush (or your fingers if you don't have one), brush the egg over each sausage roll. Sprinkle the sesame seeds, sea salt and remaining fennel seeds over the top.

Bake for 35–40 minutes or until the sausage rolls are golden brown. Cut into pieces and serve warm or at room temperature with the tomato chutney.

SERVES 4–6

QUICK TOMATO CHUTNEY

Chop 1 kg (2 lb 4 oz) tomatoes and 4 red onions. Seed and chop 2 bird's eye chillies (or to taste). Combine the tomato, onion and chilli in a large saucepan over medium heat. Stir in 1 1/4 cups (280 g) firmly packed soft brown sugar, 1 Tbsp sea salt and 2/3 cup (170 ml) apple cider vinegar. Bring to the boil and cook, stirring often (so you don't burn the base of the pan), for 40 minutes or until the chutney is thick and glossy. Divide among sterilised jars and seal. **Makes about 4 cups**

Make a double batch of these to freeze and you'll be ready to feed the hungry hordes in minutes.

OATCAKES

In my very early twenties I spent a Scottish summer working in a guesthouse on the spectacularly beautiful Isle of Mull. Every evening we served oatcakes and local stilton with pre-dinner drinks and I've loved them ever since. Especially with a slice of crunchy apple, blue cheese and a thermos of tea.

2 cups (200 g) rolled oats
1 1/3 cups (200 g) plain flour
1 Tbsp soft brown sugar
1 tsp sea salt, plus extra for sprinkling
100 g (3 1/2 oz) butter, cut into cubes

Preheat the oven to 160°C (320°F). Line two baking trays with baking paper.

Combine the oats, flour, sugar, salt and butter in the bowl of a food processor and blitz for a few seconds. Add 1/4 cup (60 ml) water and blitz again until the mixture resembles coarse sand. Add 1 tablespoon of water if necessary to bring the mixture together.

Tip the dough out onto a work surface and bring together into a disc. Roll out between two pieces of baking paper until about 3 mm (1/8 inch) thick. Cut into rounds using a 5 cm (2 inch) cutter (or thereabouts). Sprinkle with sea salt and place on the baking trays. Bake for about 20 minutes or until the oatcakes are golden. Transfer to a wire rack to cool.

MAKES ABOUT 40

QUINCE CHUTNEY

Quinces are one of my all-time favourite fruits and their aromatic, floral flavour really sings in this chutney. It's a perfect match for a creamy blue cheese and crumbly oatcakes.

1 kg (2 lb 4 oz) quinces
Juice of 2 lemons – about 1/4 cup (60 ml)
500 g (1 lb 2 oz) caster sugar
2 Tbsp yellow mustard seeds
1 tsp ground cinnamon
3 star anise
1 tsp sea salt
1 vanilla bean, split lengthways
300 ml (10 1/2 fl oz) apple cider vinegar
1 cup (250 ml) white wine

Halve and core the quinces, leaving the skin on, then cut into small cubes and place in a large heavy-based saucepan. Throw in three or four of the cores for extra pectin and colour. Pour in the lemon juice and 4 cups (1 litre) water. Bring to the boil, then reduce the heat and simmer for 1 hour or until the quinces are soft, stirring often so they don't catch on the pan. Drain, reserving the cooking liquid, and set aside.

Put the sugar, spices and salt in the empty saucepan. Scrape the vanilla seeds into the pan, add the vanilla bean and then pour in the vinegar, wine and reserved cooking liquid. Bring to a rolling boil, stirring every so often so the sugar dissolves. Cook for 5 minutes to reduce and intensify the syrup, then add the quinces. Boil for 40 minutes or until the quinces are very soft and the mixture is syrupy and turning a lovely blush pink colour. Discard the vanilla bean.

Transfer the chutney into sterilised jars and seal tightly, then turn the jars upside down to cool.

MAKES ABOUT 3 CUPS

BLACKBERRY AND ROSEMARY LOAF

This loaf is nutty, rich and delicious with a strong iced coffee around 3pm. Or any time. Swap the blackberries for any other seasonal fruit you like. I have also swirled Quince butter (page 69) through the batter before baking, which was delicious.

½ cup (100 g) *fine semolina*
1¾ cups (190 g) *hazelnut meal*
2 tsp *baking powder*
1 tsp *sea salt*
200 g (7 oz) *unsalted butter, softened*
⅔ cup (150 g) *caster sugar*
2 Tbsp *rosemary leaves, very finely chopped*
3 *eggs, at room temperature*
⅓ cup (95 g) *Greek-style yoghurt*
2 Tbsp *honey*
1 *generous handful blackberries*
1 *rosemary sprig, to decorate*

Preheat the oven to 180°C (350°F). Grease a 23 x 13 cm (9 x 5 inch) loaf tin and line with baking paper.

In a large bowl, combine the semolina, hazelnut meal, baking powder and sea salt.

Combine the butter, sugar and rosemary in the bowl of an electric mixer and beat until pale and fluffy. Add the eggs, one at a time, beating well after each addition. Gently fold in half the yoghurt and honey, then fold in half the dry ingredients. Repeat, folding until all the ingredients are well combined.

Spoon the batter into the loaf tin, smooth the surface and arrange the blackberries on top. Bake for 50 minutes or until crisp, golden and a skewer comes out clean. Let the loaf rest in the tin for 5 minutes, then gently turn out onto a tray to cool. Serve topped with a rosemary sprig.

SERVES 8

I like to serve this with yoghurt,
honey and more blackberries.

Venison shepherd's pie

Taking comfort in the season

Honey-roasted vegetables with orangey hummus ~ Venison shepherd's pie
Fig and hazelnut cobbler ~ A big jug of custard ~ Blackberry and apple crumble

Thank goodness autumn is here. Finally there's a chill in the air, and the summer sun's blinding glare has given way to a gentle light, a settling of the dust and an excuse to use the oven again. It's time to dig out the soft woollen blankets and dive into crumbles and custards, roasts and pies. This collection of recipes is an ode to all of the above, to the reprieve autumn brings and the baking and sharing of comfort foods for cooler days.

HONEY-ROASTED VEGETABLES
WITH ORANGEY HUMMUS

A rainbow of vegetables, roasted with a little honey, can stand alone as a fabulous main meal, especially when served on a bed of delicious hummus and alongside a peppery rocket (arugula) salad. This is also a good side dish for roasted or barbecued meats and absolutely begs for some warm Turkish bread or other flatbread.

The vegetables I used here were grown by Erika (who is pictured on page 18) and her partner Hayden. They grow organic produce from their plot at the base of the Blue Mountains. I am ever in awe of their commitment to, and love of, what they do, and you can taste that love in every crunchy carrot and radish. You can find Erika's kraut recipe on page 70.

1 bunch baby radishes
2 bunches baby carrots (different colours if you can find them)
1 bunch baby beetroot
Juice of 1 lemon
2 Tbsp honey
2 Tbsp olive oil
1 tsp sea salt

Orangey hummus
³/₄ cup (145 g) dried chickpeas, soaked overnight in cold water then cooked until tender, or 400 g (14 oz) tin chickpeas, rinsed and drained
¹/₃ cup (90 g) tahini
Grated zest of 1 orange
¹/₄ cup (60 ml) freshly squeezed orange juice
2 garlic cloves
1 tsp sea salt
¹/₂ tsp ground cumin

Preheat the oven to 200°C (400°F). Line a large baking tray with baking paper.

Trim the vegetables and halve or quarter any large radishes or beetroot. Combine the vegetables on the tray and drizzle with the lemon juice, honey and olive oil. Sprinkle with the sea salt and some freshly ground black pepper and roast for 30 minutes or until the vegetables are soft and beginning to brown.

Meanwhile, to make the hummus, combine the chickpeas in a food processor with the tahini, orange zest, orange juice, garlic, sea salt and cumin. Blitz until the hummus has a lovely smooth consistency, adding a little iced water if it's too thick. Check the seasoning, adjust to taste and serve, or store in the fridge for up to a fortnight.

To serve, spread the hummus over a large plate and top with the warm roasted vegetables.

SERVES 6

VENISON SHEPHERD'S PIE

Like all good, simple fare, this pie's deliciousness is all thanks to the sum of its parts – a base of tasty soffritto, good-quality meat minced by hand and a light, fluffy potato topping. You could speed it up by skipping the long slow soffritto step and just sweating the onion, carrot and celery for 10 minutes or until soft and translucent. And you could also just buy pre-minced meat. The end result will still be lovely.

I am of course biased because we produce venison here on our farm, but truly this is the most wonderful of meats. Lean, full of delicate flavour and so easy to cook, please do try it whenever you get the opportunity. Here, venison brings an extra level of luxury to this simple, wonderful pie, but you could also stick with tradition and make this with minced lamb, or even minced beef (which is known as a cottage pie).

3 brown onions, diced
2 carrots, peeled and diced
2 celery stalks
¼ cup (60 ml) olive oil
700 g (1 lb 9 oz) venison topside
  or rump
150 g (5½ oz) butter
1 Tbsp thyme leaves
400 ml (14 fl oz) beef stock
1 Tbsp cornflour
2 Tbsp Worcestershire sauce
2 Tbsp tomato paste (concentrated
  purée)
1 kg (2 lb 4 oz) floury potatoes
¼ cup (60 ml) milk

First start the soffritto. Combine the onion, carrot, celery and olive oil in a saucepan over low heat. Cook for 2 hours, stirring every now and then, until the mixture is a thick, dark-brown paste.

Meanwhile, cut the venison into small, pea-sized pieces. Doing this by hand takes about 10 minutes, but you could ask your butcher or use a food processor or mincer if you have one.

Melt 20 g (¾ oz) of the butter in a large heavy-based saucepan over medium–high heat. Add the venison and thyme and cook, stirring often, until the venison is browned all over. Whisk together the beef stock and cornflour and add to the venison with the soffritto, Worcestershire sauce and tomato paste. Stir well, bring to a simmer and cook over low heat for 40 minutes. Season to taste.

While the meat is cooking, peel and cut the potatoes into small cubes. Place in a large saucepan and cover with cold water. Cook over high heat until the potato is completely tender when pierced with a fork. Drain and mash with 50 g (1¾ oz) of the butter and the milk.

Preheat the oven to 180°C (350°F). Transfer the meat mixture to an ovenproof dish and top with the mashed potato (I sometimes add it in clumps, which seems to help it crunch up during baking). Dot the top with the remaining butter and bake for 45 minutes or until the potato is golden and the meat is bubbling. Serve with a simple green salad.

A NOTE ON THE SOFFRITTO
Soffritto is a recipe base, usually of carrot, celery and onion cooked long and slow in olive oil, versions of which play a big part in Italian, French, Spanish and South American cooking. Although it is cooked for 2 hours in this recipe, most of that time is completely hands off and the result is an intense flavour bomb that will bring goodness to any soup, casserole, braise or pasta sauce you use it in. Make a double batch and freeze it in ice-cube trays for easy flavour access.

SERVES 6–8

FIG AND HAZELNUT COBBLER

I can't think of a more delicious dish to make and serve or give people for a cool Sunday morning in autumn. Swap the figs with any other seasonal fruit you like; poached quinces, pears or rhubarb would be gorgeous, as would stone fruit or berries. You could also serve the cobbler as a pudding with the custard from page 24.

80 g (2¾ oz) butter, melted,
 plus extra for greasing
½ cup (75 g) plain flour
½ cup (75 g) wholemeal plain flour
½ cup (110 g) golden caster sugar,
 plus a little extra for sprinkling
1½ tsp baking powder
A pinch of sea salt
½ cup (125 ml) buttermilk
2 eggs
1 tsp vanilla bean paste
Grated zest of 1 orange
8 figs, quartered
1 cup (135 g) toasted hazelnuts,
 roughly chopped
Honey, for drizzling
Greek-style yoghurt, to serve

Preheat the oven to 170°C (340°F). Use a little butter to grease a large ovenproof dish.

Whisk together the flours, sugar, baking powder and sea salt in a large bowl. In a jug, whisk together the buttermilk, melted butter, eggs, vanilla and orange zest.

Fold the wet and dry ingredients together until just combined, then pour into the dish, top with the figs and sprinkle with a little extra sugar. Bake for 25 minutes or until the batter is golden but still a little wobbly (don't overcook or it will dry out).

Sprinkle the hazelnuts over the cobbler and drizzle with a little honey. Serve warm with thick Greek-style yoghurt.

SERVES 6

A BIG JUG OF CUSTARD

Combine 1¼ cups (310 ml) milk and 1¼ cups (310 ml) single (pure) cream in a saucepan over medium–high heat. Split a vanilla bean lengthways and scrape the seeds into the pan. Add the vanilla bean and heat until the mixture is almost boiling.

Whisk ⅓ cup (75 g) caster sugar, 1 Tbsp cornflour and 6 egg yolks until pale and creamy. Splash a little of the warm milk mixture into the egg mixture and whisk again, then pour in the remaining milk mixture. Mix well, then return the whole lot to the saucepan. Stir over low heat for 5 minutes or until the custard is just about coating the back of your wooden spoon. Discard the vanilla bean, pour into a jug and store in the fridge until ready to serve.
Makes about 3 cups

BLACKBERRY AND APPLE CRUMBLE

This recipe makes more than you'll need for one crumble, and this is because I'd love you to set aside half the crumble mixture and pop it in the freezer. That means you are only ever a few unpeeled apples away from having a gorgeous crumble in the oven. Also, it makes a wonderful topping for all kinds of cakes – sprinkle a cup or so over the top of my sturdy picnic cake (page 55) before baking, for example. You can also spread it over a baking tray and bake until crunchy, then use it as a rich granola-style topping for ice cream, roasted fruit, yoghurt and fresh fruit for breakfast, and so on.

Depending on availability and taste, please go ahead and swap the blackberries with any other berry and the apple with poached quinces or stewed plums. And the hazelnuts could move aside for almonds, walnuts, pecans or a combination of all three.

Regarding what to serve crumble with, my feeling (for what it is worth) is always and only custard. Whether to serve this hot or cold has been a cause of ongoing debate in my house and we've settled it with the mandate that a hot pudding should be set down with a chilled custard and vice versa.

6 cooking apples, peeled, cored and
   thinly sliced
2 cups (260 g) blackberries
Grated zest and juice of 1 orange
2 Tbsp caster sugar

Crumble topping
280 g (10 oz) unsalted butter
2 cups (300 g) plain flour
1 cup (220 g) firmly packed soft
   brown sugar
1/4 tsp ground cinnamon
A pinch of salt
3/4 cup (115 g) toasted hazelnuts
1 1/3 cups (135 g) rolled oats

Preheat the oven to 180°C (350°F).

For the crumble topping, combine the butter, flour, brown sugar, cinnamon, salt and hazelnuts in the bowl of a food processor and blitz for a few seconds, until just combined. (Or combine in a large bowl and work together with your fingertips until coarse and lumpy.) Add the oats and mix well. If you're freezing any of the crumble mixture, transfer it to a container or snap-lock bag now and then pop it into the freezer.

Spread the crumble mixture over a couple of baking trays and bake for 20 minutes or until just beginning to turn golden. Toss it around halfway through cooking so nothing gets stuck on the trays.

Meanwhile, prepare the fruit. Combine the apples, blackberries, orange zest, orange juice, caster sugar and 2 tablespoons water in a saucepan. Cover and cook over medium–low heat for 10 minutes, stirring halfway through, or until the fruit is tender.

Transfer the fruit mixture to an ovenproof dish – the size depends on how deep you like your crumble, but I generally use a 30 cm (12 inch) enamel roasting tin that's 5 cm (2 inches) deep. Sprinkle the roasted crumble mixture over the fruit and bake for 20 minutes.

SERVES 6–8

Out for lunch

Menu 1: Pasta salad with olive and walnut pesto ~ Smoky zucchini and chilli hummus with pita bread ~ Baci di dama

Menu 2: Crunchy fennel and apple salad ~ Triple-ginger loaf

Menu 3: Tomato, capsicum and pearl couscous salad ~ Sweet and salty trail mix

My time working with Slow Food in Italy was such an eye-opener in terms of how we eat lunch at work. I'd just come from a busy office in Sydney where most of us would eat one-handed at our desks, barely paying attention to what we were actually ingesting, all the while staring at the computer screen. When I recounted this scenario to my Italian friends they first expressed sympathy for our sad existence, then moved to disapproval about this unsophisticated waste of a mealtime experience.

I know this isn't true of all Italian offices, but where I worked, everyone left the office at lunch for at least half an hour (and usually more like one to one and a half hours). We'd have a meal, at home or the nearby cafe, then finish with a coffee and more conversation before going back to work. And work we did – better I think, for having had such a good break.

These days I work from home, sharing the farm office with my husband, Tim. Too often we quickly throw something together before rushing back to our desks to eat. But it makes a huge difference to the afternoon's productivity if we take even 20 minutes to sit in the sun and slowly eat lunch. This menu is a reminder to myself to do that more often, and an encouragement to you to do the same. Surely we can all spare 20 minutes away from our desks to refuel? Better yet, imagine how happy it would make someone if you made them a 'not-sad desk lunch' and invited them to the park to eat with you.

PASTA SALAD WITH OLIVE AND WALNUT PESTO

This is a really tasty pasta salad that packs lots of flavour and tastes great cold. I also suggest making a double batch of the pesto because it goes beautifully with practically anything. Serve it as a dip, with barbecued meats, dolloped on top of a vegetable soup or stirred into a simple brown rice bowl with a few extra vegetables for a fast lunch.

500 g (1 lb 2 oz) wholemeal pasta spirals
2 handfuls baby English spinach
Flaked or grated parmesan cheese, to serve
Chilli flakes, to taste

Olive and walnut pesto
$1/2$ cup (90 g) green olives, pitted and roughly chopped
$1/2$ cup (60 g) walnuts, toasted and roughly chopped
2 garlic cloves, roughly chopped
1 handful mint leaves
1 Tbsp white miso paste
Juice of 1 lemon
$1/4$ cup (60 ml) olive oil

Cook the pasta according to the packet instructions.

Meanwhile, for the pesto, combine the chopped olives and walnuts with the garlic, mint, miso paste and lemon juice in a large mortar and pestle or food processor and bash or blitz until you have a coarse paste. Loosen the pesto with the olive oil.

Drain the pasta, reserving $1/4$ cup (60 ml) of the cooking water. Stir the pesto through the warm pasta, adding a little of the cooking water if it looks dry. Fold the spinach through the pasta, season to taste and top with the parmesan and chilli flakes. Serve immediately or pop in the fridge for up to 2 days.

SERVES 4

SMOKY ZUCCHINI AND CHILLI HUMMUS

There is so much to love about this recipe. It's a wonderfully not-boring way to use up a glut of zucchini, and it's really versatile. Use it as a dip or give it a more prominent role as a base for sliced cherry tomatoes drizzled with olive oil, or as a bed for barbecued chicken or pan-fried fish. I also love to dollop some on top of some brown rice along with a handful of greens and some hot-smoked salmon as a super-quick grain bowl.

6 zucchini (courgettes), cut into rough chunks
$1/3$ cup (80 ml) olive oil
$1/2$ tsp chilli flakes
$1/2$ tsp sea salt, or to taste
1 Tbsp tahini
Juice of 1 lemon
2 Tbsp Greek-style yoghurt

Preheat the oven to 200°C (400°F). Put the zucchini chunks in a roasting tin, drizzle with half of the olive oil and sprinkle with the chilli flakes, sea salt and some freshly ground black pepper. Roast for 40 minutes or until the zucchini is soft and beginning to caramelise and darken around the edges.

Transfer the zucchini to a blender or food processor, scraping as much from the base of the tin as possible (this gives colour and flavour). Add the tahini, lemon juice and remaining olive oil and blitz until smooth. Stir in the yoghurt and season to taste. Store in the fridge for up to a week.

MAKES ABOUT 1$1/2$ CUPS

CRUNCHY FENNEL AND APPLE SALAD

Pack this gorgeous, crunchy autumn salad (pictured on page 27) with a piece of chewy baguette or sourdough to mop up the lovely dressing. Consider making a double batch of the dressing – it's lovely with any green salad.

2 fennel bulbs, trimmed
1/4 white cabbage, trimmed
2 granny smith apples
1/2 cup (75 g) hazelnuts, toasted
   and roughly chopped
2 Tbsp dill leaves, finely chopped

Buttermilk dressing
1/4 cup (60 ml) buttermilk
2 Tbsp Greek-style yoghurt
Juice of 1 lemon
1 tsp dijon mustard

Thinly slice the fennel, cabbage and apples (I use a mandolin). Combine with the hazelnuts and dill in a bowl.

Combine the dressing ingredients in a jar and shake well to combine.

Mix the dressing with the salad and season to taste.

SERVES 4

TOMATO, CAPSICUM AND PEARL COUSCOUS SALAD

Full of colour and flavour, this vegetarian salad is the antithesis of a sad desk lunch. Pack it up with some fresh seasonal fruit and a handful of Sweet and salty trail mix (page 33) and you'll really be looking forward to lunchtime.

2 red capsicums (peppers)
2 yellow capsicums (peppers)
8 tomatoes, halved
Olive oil, for drizzling
Sea salt
1 1/3 cups (250 g) pearl couscous
2 cups (500 ml) boiling water
2/3 cup (100 g) crumbled feta cheese
2 Tbsp pine nuts, toasted

Dressing
1/4 cup (60 ml) red wine vinegar
1/4 cup (60 ml) olive oil
2 Tbsp sesame seeds, toasted
2 Tbsp nigella seeds
1 tsp ground cumin

Preheat the oven to 200°C (400°F). Cut the red and yellow capsicums into quarters, removing the seeds, and place on a baking tray. Put the tomato halves on another baking tray. Drizzle the vegetables with olive oil and sprinkle with sea salt. Pop the capsicums in the oven for 30 minutes, then add the tomatoes and roast for a further 20 minutes or until the capsicums are completely softened and beginning to blacken around the edges.

Meanwhile, put the couscous and boiling water in a saucepan over medium–high heat. Cook for 8 minutes or until the couscous is tender and most of the water has been absorbed. Cover the pan with a tea towel.

Mix together the dressing ingredients and season well.

Use a fork to stir the dressing through the couscous, then gently fold in the roasted capsicum and tomato. Sprinkle with the feta and toasted pine nuts. Serve immediately or store in the fridge for up to 3 days.

SERVES 4–6

Imagine how happy it would make someone if you gave them this 'not-sad desk lunch'.

VARIATION
Instead of sandwiching these together, you could melt some white, milk or dark chocolate and either dip the cookies into the chocolate or drizzle them with chocolate on the trays.

BACI DI DAMA

Baci di dama are gorgeous little hazelnut and chocolate biscuits from Piedmont, the north-western pocket of Italy that I called home for some years. The area is known for growing beautiful hazelnuts (it claims to be the home of Nutella), and every cafe and patisserie in the region sells baci di dama (ladies' kisses) by weight. I remember friends coming over to dinner with little waxed bags of baci di dama to share with coffee.

Bring a bag of these and a coffee to work for an extra nice colleague and it will make his or her day. They are a touch crumbly while still warm, so be gentle with them. Good fresh hazelnuts are the key here.

1 cup (135 g) hazelnuts, toasted
  and skinned
3/4 cup (130 g) rice flour
2 Tbsp plain flour or gluten-free
  plain flour
100 g (3 1/2 oz) chilled butter,
  cut into cubes
2 Tbsp ice-cold water
1/3 cup (75 g) caster sugar
1/2 cup (75 g) chopped dark
  chocolate

Using a food processor, blitz the hazelnuts into a fine meal. Add the rice flour, plain flour, butter, water and sugar. Blitz for about 10 seconds or until the mixture is just coming together. Turn out onto a work surface and bring together into a rough dough. Form the dough into a disc, wrap in plastic wrap and place in the fridge to chill for 30 minutes.

Preheat the oven to 180°C (350°F). Line two large baking trays with baking paper.

Pull out a piece of dough about the size of a marble, roll it into a ball between your hands and place on one of the trays. Repeat with the remaining dough. Bake the cookies for 10 minutes or until just golden brown. Transfer to a wire rack to cool.

Melt the chocolate in a heatproof bowl over a saucepan of simmering water. Spoon a little onto a cookie and sandwich with another cookie, then repeat with the remaining cookies.

MAKES ABOUT 20

SWEET AND SALTY TRAIL MIX

Trail mix is great for work snacks, car trips and, of course, as sustenance when out trail walking. Combine 1 cup (160 g) oven-roasted almonds, 1 cup (45 g) pretzels, 1/2 cup (75 g) pepitas (pumpkin seeds), 1/2 cup (110 g) crystallised ginger, 1/2 cup (75 g) dried cranberries and 1 cup (140 g) roughly chopped white chocolate.

TRIPLE-GINGER LOAF

This loaf is for my mother, Annie, who adores ginger in everything, and lots of it. It's not super sweet, but dark and almost spicy thanks to the triple ginger hit (ground, fresh and crystallised ginger) and the molasses. We love it with a scrape of butter and some tart jam but it's also great with a lemony cream cheese frosting, flying solo or toasted and topped with the lemon curd from page 75. I'd quite fancy this for dessert or a posh brunch: toast a fairly thin slice or two and serve it with a poached pear or quince half, a dollop of thick cream, a drizzle of poaching liquid and a sprinkle of Sweet dukkah (page 75).

3/4 cup (110 g) plain flour
2/3 cup (100 g) wholemeal plain flour
1 tsp baking powder
2 tsp ground ginger
1/2 tsp ground cinnamon
1/2 tsp mixed spice
A good pinch of cayenne pepper
A good pinch of salt
100 g (3 1/2 oz) butter, softened
1/3 cup (75 g) firmly packed soft brown sugar
1 Tbsp honey
3 eggs
2 Tbsp molasses
2 Tbsp boiling water
1 tsp bicarbonate of soda
1/4 cup (60 ml) buttermilk
1/4 cup (50 g) grated fresh ginger
1/2 cup (110 g) crystallised ginger, roughly chopped

Preheat the oven to 180°C (350°F). Grease a large loaf tin, about 30 cm (12 inches) long, and line with baking paper.

Sift together the flours, baking powder, spices and salt in a large bowl.

Put the butter, brown sugar and honey in the bowl of an electric mixer and beat until pale and creamy, at least 4 minutes. Add the eggs, one at a time, beating well after each addition.

In a third bowl, stir the molasses, boiling water and bicarbonate of soda together. Leave for a minute for it to froth up a bit, then pour into the butter mixture and mix for a couple of minutes.

Fold in the dry ingredients, then add the buttermilk. Mix to combine, then fold in the fresh and crystallised ginger. Spoon the batter into the tin and smooth the top, then bake for 45 minutes or until the loaf feels springy and has begun to pull away from the sides of the tin.

SERVES 8

MORE IDEAS FOR GOING OUT (OF THE OFFICE) FOR LUNCH

~ Simple harira soup (page 39)
~ Lisa's frittata (page 44)
~ Comforting chicken and veggie casserole (page 46)
~ Pearl barley, beetroot and yoghurt salad (page 52)
~ Dark chocolate, ginger and almond clusters (page 56)

Mind the gap

Spiced chia and smoothie puddings ~ Simple harira soup ~ Peanut butter muesli bars

The first few weeks of breastfeeding were marked – for me, at least – by crazy attacks of hunger. I'd be up at 3am feeding and all of a sudden be rocked by waves of hunger. The kind that could take out a whole fridge in its wake.

Sometimes you just need fast, filling food. Sometimes you are too tired or distracted to feed yourself properly, and it's helpful in those moments to have something filling, wholesome and tasty at hand. This minimises the possibility of eating a whole block of dodgy cooking chocolate out of desperation and means you are still giving your body the fuel it needs. So, if you have a friend home with a new baby, heavy heart or recovering body, consider making them some super-filling and nutritious treats like these to keep handy.

SPICED CHIA AND SMOOTHIE PUDDINGS

Chia seeds are full of goodness and are also very filling, ideal for anyone who's in need of nourishing food. Instead of topping the puddings with the blueberry smoothie, try adding Apple butter (page 68) or Rhubarb compote (page 74). You could also use berries or sliced peaches.

3 cups (750 ml) almond milk
  (page 74 or store bought) or
  cow's milk
$1/2$ cup (100 g) white chia seeds
$1/2$ tsp ground cinnamon
$1/4$ tsp ground nutmeg
$1/2$ tsp vanilla bean paste
1 Tbsp maple syrup or honey
Sweet dukkah (page 75) and dried
  rose petals, to serve (optional)

Blueberry smoothie
1 cup (155 g) fresh or frozen
  blueberries
1 banana (preferably frozen)
10 walnuts
1 Tbsp coconut oil
3 cm ($1^1/4$ inch) piece ginger
4 ice cubes

Put the milk, chia seeds, cinnamon, nutmeg, vanilla and maple syrup into a jug and whisk to combine. Leave for 10 minutes to thicken up a little, then divide the mixture among four jars or glasses. Place the puddings in the fridge for 30 minutes.

To make the smoothie, combine all of the ingredients in a high-powered blender with 1 cup (250 ml) water and whizz until smooth.

Spoon the smoothie over the top of the puddings and return them to the fridge until ready to serve.

Just before serving, sprinkle the chia puddings with the dukkah and rose petals, if using.

SERVES 4

Try topping the puddings with apple butter, rhubarb compote, berries or sliced peaches.

SIMPLE HARIRA SOUP

A pared-down take on the classic Moroccan harira, which is traditionally served during Ramadan, this is a gorgeous, filling and healthy soup. I've been making it for lunch at workshops and at home for many years. You can leave out the chicken or replace it with diced lamb shoulder.

1 Tbsp (20 g) butter
1 brown onion, diced
1 tsp ground cumin
1 tsp ground turmeric
$^1/_2$ tsp ground cinnamon
600 g (1 lb 5 oz) chicken thigh
    fillets, chopped
2 x 400 g (14 oz) tins chopped
    tomatoes
400 g (14 oz) tin chickpeas, or
    $^3/_4$ cup (145 g) dried chickpeas,
    soaked overnight in cold water
    then cooked until tender
$^1/_2$ cup (100 g) red lentils
1 cup (20 g) flat-leaf parsley leaves,
    plus extra to serve
1 cup (30 g) coriander (cilantro)
    leaves, plus extra to serve
3 cups (750 ml) chicken stock
Turkish bread, to serve

Melt the butter in a heavy-based saucepan over medium–high heat. Cook the onion for 5 minutes or until soft and translucent. Add the spices and chopped chicken and cook, stirring often, for 5 minutes.

Stir in the tomatoes, chickpeas, lentils, herbs and stock. Gently simmer for about 30 minutes. Serve the soup with some warm Turkish bread and a few extra parsley and coriander leaves.

SERVES 8

PEANUT BUTTER MUESLI BARS

I made batch after batch of these when both Alice and Tom were newborns. They were my salvation and I guarded my stash jealously. Once Tim had a fencing contractor in for morning tea and they polished off half a jar at once. I came home from a shopping trip in town, starving, with a screaming baby in tow, and found the jar empty. With hindsight, I can admit my reaction was disproportionately angry.

It took me a while to come up with a muesli bar recipe that wasn't too soft and chewy, and that could hold together in a lunch box or jar and this is it. The key is using an egg white to bind the ingredients together and add some extra crunch.

2 cups (200 g) rolled oats
1 cup (160 g) almonds
1/2 cup (60 g) walnuts
1 cup (155 g) pepitas (pumpkin seeds)
1/2 cup (75 g) sesame seeds
1 cup (55 g) flaked coconut
1/2 cup (175 g) honey
1/3 cup (75 g) firmly packed soft brown sugar
3/4 cup (215 g) peanut butter (the good, natural kind if possible)
1 Tbsp coconut oil
1 large egg white, whisked until frothy
1/2 tsp sea salt
1/2 cup (40 g) wheatgerm
1 cup (170 g) raisins, dried cranberries, apricots or figs, roughly chopped

Preheat the oven to 160°C (320°F). Grease and line a 38 x 26 x 3 cm (15 x 10½ x 1¼ inch) cake tin with baking paper.

Combine the oats, almonds, walnuts, seeds and coconut on a baking tray and bake for about 15 minutes or until the coconut is just turning golden. Tip the mixture into a large mixing bowl.

Combine the honey, brown sugar, peanut butter and coconut oil in a small saucepan and bring just to the boil. Reduce the heat and cook, stirring often, for 5 minutes. Remove from the heat and set aside to cool for 10 minutes.

Stir the beaten egg white and salt into the honey mixture, then pour into the oat mixture, stir in the wheatgerm and dried fruit and mix well. Scrape the mixture into the cake tin and bake for 35 minutes or until golden brown. Leave to cool in the tin before cutting into bars or squares.

MAKES ABOUT 12

MORE IDEAS FOR MINDING THE GAP

~ *Apple, fennel and pork sausage rolls (page 12)*
~ *Oatcakes (page 15) with blue cheese*
~ *Orangey hummus (page 20) or Smoky zucchini and chilli hummus (page 29), with a few snap-lock bags of carrot sticks, celery sticks and other crunchy vegetables*
~ *Crunchy fennel and apple salad (page 30)*
~ *Comforting chicken and veggie casserole (page 46)*
~ *Granola and choc-chip cookies (page 47)*
~ *Jars of Bircher muesli (page 63)*

I made batch after batch of these when both Alice and Tom were newborns.

Packed lunches

Lisa's frittata ~ Comforting chicken and veggie casserole with buttered rice
Granola and choc-chip cookies

Writing this book has brought about many emotional and humbling moments. I've had a number of conversations with friends, Mum, my sister, sisters-in-law and online community about what kinds of care packages they have received and given in times of trouble or illness. In all of these stories I hear, over and over again, just how generous people are in times of others' need.

One friend told me how much it meant to her family when, having just moved to the area, she became very sick and had to spend six weeks in hospital while her husband and three small children waited anxiously back home on the farm. Almost instantly, a group of parents from their new school organised a meal roster. Participants were asked to drop meals in a cool box at the school office by 3pm each day, so her husband or whoever was collecting the kids could also pick up dinner. People they hardly knew, teachers from the school and friends of friends kicked in and contributed everything from casseroles to soups to pre-paid take-away dinners. Perhaps the most useful gift of all was items to pack in school lunch boxes. Between worry for his partner, keeping the farm on track and caring for three unsettled little people, her husband was completely stretched. Having healthy lunch boxes sorted was a huge help.

Next time you make something for a friend who is going through a difficult time, consider giving them a solution to that ever-present quandary: 'What on earth am I going to put in the lunch boxes?' A simple question that seems so much more of a headache when life is smacking you around a bit.

LISA'S FRITTATA

Lisa Darley is one half of Kurrafalls Farm, a beautiful property just 10 minutes away from us. Here, she and partner Quenten raise pastured chooks, Dorper sheep and two gorgeous children. With its layers of veggies, loads of eggs, cheese, potatoes and spinach, Lisa's frittata is one big beautiful meal in one.

My kids devour this for Sunday night dinner, so I usually make two frittatas, and freeze one in slices for school lunches. Final point in favour of this frittata: it's a great way to clean out the bottom of the fridge, so add any vegetables you find lurking in there – mushrooms, zucchini (courgettes), tomatoes or even roasted sweet potato.

2 sebago potatoes, about 400 g (14 oz)
2 Tbsp olive oil
1 red onion, chopped
70 g (2½ oz) pancetta, chopped
2¼ cups (100 g) baby English spinach
1⅔ cups (200 g) red grape tomatoes, halved
1 red capsicum (pepper), chopped
8 eggs
½ cup (125 ml) thick (double) cream
½ cup (40 g) shredded parmesan cheese
¼ cup (25 g) grated cheddar cheese
¼ cup (35 g) crumbled feta cheese

Preheat the oven to 200°C (400°F). Lightly grease a 5 cm (2 inch) deep ovenproof dish, 26 x 16 cm (10½ x 6¼ inches) or thereabouts – I often use a fairly deep, 30 cm (12 inch) ovenproof frying pan.

Put the potatoes in a small saucepan, cover with water and cook for about 15 minutes or until tender right through when pierced with a skewer or fork. Allow to cool, then thinly slice.

Meanwhile, heat the olive oil in a non-stick frying pan over medium heat. Cook the onion for 3 minutes. Add the pancetta and cook, stirring, for 3–4 minutes or until the onion is tender and the pancetta is golden. Add the spinach and cook for 1 minute or until the spinach has just wilted. Combine the onion mixture, tomatoes and capsicum in a bowl.

Arrange half the potato slices in a single layer in the prepared dish or pan and top with half the onion mixture. Repeat with the remaining potato and onion mixture.

Whisk the eggs and cream in a bowl. Gently pour the mixture over the vegetable mixture and sprinkle with the parmesan, cheddar and feta cheeses. Bake for 30–35 minutes or until the frittata is set and the top is golden. Stand for 5 minutes before slicing.

SERVES 6

My kids devour this for
Sunday night dinner.

COMFORTING CHICKEN AND
VEGGIE CASSEROLE WITH BUTTERED RICE

¼ cup (35 g) plain flour
⅓ cup (80 ml) olive oil
1 whole chicken, cut into 8 pieces,
 or 6–8 chicken thigh pieces
1 leek, pale part only, thinly sliced
1 carrot, peeled and finely diced
1 celery stalk, finely diced
1 red capsicum (pepper), finely chopped
1 garlic clove, peeled
1 tsp thyme leaves
1 tsp sage leaves, finely chopped
1 tsp rosemary leaves, finely chopped
1 tsp sweet paprika
1 Tbsp tomato paste (concentrated purée)
400 g (14 oz) tin whole tomatoes
2 cups (500 ml) chicken stock

Buttered rice
1 cup (200 g) jasmine rice
60 g (2¼ oz) butter
A good pinch of salt

On cold school days, when the kids need something undemanding and familiar, I pack them this nourishing casserole in thermos flasks. The flavours are simple and the texture is soft. It's basically a hug in a thermos.

Season the flour with salt and pepper and place in a shallow bowl. Heat a little of the olive oil in a large saucepan over medium–high heat. Toss the chicken pieces in the flour and then brown, in batches, until each side has a lovely golden colour. Transfer the chicken to a plate.

Reduce the heat to medium–low, add a little more olive oil and cook the leek, carrot, celery, capsicum, garlic, thyme, sage and rosemary for 10 minutes or until soft. Stir in the paprika and tomato paste and cook for another minute. Return the chicken pieces to the pan and pour in the tomatoes and stock. Cover, turn the heat down as low as it will go and leave to cook for 1 hour or until tender.

For the buttered rice, cook the jasmine rice according to the packet instructions (I use the absorption method). Once cooked, stir through the butter and salt.

Serve the hot casserole with the buttered rice. If you're packing it in a thermos, do so while it's nice and hot – shred the chicken from the bones and mix it with the tomato sauce and vegetables on a bed of buttered rice.

SERVES 4–6

GRANOLA AND CHOC-CHIP COOKIES

These cookies are wholesome, absolutely delicious and stayers (by which I mean they last well in a jar or airtight container). I've been making them for years – I absolutely love them and hope you will too. If you're making these for kids to take to school, you might want to use a nut-free granola.

150 g (5¹/₂ oz) butter, softened
¹/₄ cup (55 g) caster sugar
¹/₂ cup (110 g) firmly packed soft brown sugar
1 egg
1 tsp natural vanilla extract
1²/₃ cups (250 g) wholemeal plain flour
1 tsp baking powder
1 cup (125 g) granola
¹/₂ cup (85 g) milk chocolate chips

Preheat the oven to 180°C (350°F). Line two large baking trays with baking paper.

Combine the butter and sugars in the bowl of an electric mixer and beat until light and fluffy. Add the egg and vanilla and mix until well combined. Fold in the flour, baking powder, granola and chocolate chips.

Roll the mixture into balls about the size of a walnut and place on the trays, leaving space between them so they can spread. Flatten a little with a fork, then bake for 15 minutes or until golden. Leave to cool on a wire rack. If the cookies are a little soft in the middle for your taste, pop them back in the oven for another 5–10 minutes so they crisp up and keep well without going soggy. Store in a jar or airtight container.

MAKES ABOUT 24

MORE IDEAS FOR PACKED LUNCHES

~ Apple, fennel and pork sausage rolls (page 12)
~ Blackberry and rosemary loaf (page 16)
~ Make the wholemeal pancakes from page 63, but make them smaller, then spread one with butter and jam or Apple butter (page 68) and sandwich it with another

Autumn picnic by the river

Eggplant and tomato bake with crème fraîche ~ Pearl barley, beetroot and yoghurt salad
Piedmontese capsicums ~ Wholemeal apple and marmalade cake (aka the good, sturdy picnic cake)
Dark chocolate, ginger and almond clusters ~ Salted peanut and white chocolate cookies

All these recipes are good served at room temperature and all travel well,
which means they are not only perfect picnic fare but also excellent candidates
for dishes to make and give away to friends or family who might need
a 'love bomb' left on their doorstep.

This bake is rich and creamy yet
full of zingy, punchy flavours.

EGGPLANT AND TOMATO BAKE
WITH CRÈME FRAÎCHE

4 eggplant (aubergines), sliced into 1 cm (1/2 inch) rounds
2 tsp salt
2 Tbsp olive oil
1 brown onion, diced
4 garlic cloves, roughly chopped
1.5 kg (3 lb 5 oz) tomatoes, roughly chopped,
    or 3 x 400 g (14 oz) tins chopped tomatoes
1 handful basil, roughly chopped
1/4 cup (60 ml) vegetable oil
1 cup (100 g) finely grated parmesan cheese
300 g (10 1/2 oz) crème fraîche (page 74 or store bought)
Grated zest of 1 lemon
1/2 cup (30 g) fresh breadcrumbs (made from sourdough, if possible)

I absolutely love this dish: it's rich and creamy yet full of zingy, punchy flavours, and takes full advantage of early autumn's abundance of tomatoes and eggplant. Delicious warm or at room temperature, you can make it in advance, then serve it with a green salad as a main or with grilled meat as a side dish. If you're cooking for vegetarians or friends who you suspect have had their fill of lasagne, give this a try. If you find crème fraîche elusive or costly, either make it yourself using the recipe on page 74, swap it for sour cream, or replace it with 250 g (9 oz) ricotta cheese mixed with 1/4 cup (25 g) grated parmesan cheese and an egg.

Put the eggplant slices in a large colander and sprinkle with the salt. Set aside for 1 hour, then rinse and pat dry with paper towel.

Preheat the oven to 180°C (350°F). Lightly grease a large ovenproof dish, approximately 30 x 20 x 8 cm (12 x 8 x 3 1/4 inches).

Heat the olive oil in a large saucepan over medium–high heat. Cook the onion until translucent (about 5 minutes), then add the garlic and cook for 1 minute. Tip in the chopped tomatoes and basil, reduce the heat and cook, stirring often, for 20 minutes.

Meanwhile, heat the vegetable oil in a large frying pan and, working in batches, fry the eggplant until soft and golden on each side, topping up with more oil if needed – there should be about 2 mm (1/16 inch) of oil in the pan at all times. This can feel like a bit of a punish, but it's the only messy part and definitely worth it!

Place a layer of eggplant in the ovenproof dish and top with a third of the tomato sauce. Sprinkle with a quarter of the parmesan and repeat so you have three layers of eggplant, tomato and parmesan. To finish, whisk together the crème fraîche, lemon zest and remaining 1/4 cup (25 g) parmesan. Spread this mixture over the top of the eggplant and tomato, then sprinkle with the breadcrumbs. Bake for 30 minutes or until the top is golden brown. Serve warm or at room temperature.

SERVES 6–8

PEARL BARLEY, BEETROOT AND YOGHURT SALAD

A really yummy, healthy and easy salad, this one is great for a picnic or buffet lunch as it sits around happily for ages and tastes great at room temperature. You can replace the beetroot with another roast vegetable if you prefer.

3 beetroot, cut into quarters
1/2 cup (125 ml) olive oil
1 1/2 cups (300 g) pearl barley
6 cups (1.5 litres) boiling water
2 Tbsp apple cider vinegar
Grated zest and juice of 1 lemon
1/4 cup (40 g) sunflower seeds
1/4 cup (40 g) pine nuts
1 bunch dill, finely chopped
1 cup (260 g) Greek-style yoghurt

Preheat the oven to 200°C (400°F). Put the beetroot quarters on a baking tray, drizzle with a little of the olive oil and sprinkle with salt and pepper. Roast for 40 minutes or until tender.

Meanwhile, combine the barley and 2 tablespoons of the olive oil in a large saucepan over medium–high heat. Toast, stirring often, for 10 minutes. Pour in the boiling water and boil until tender, about 15 minutes.

Mix together the remaining olive oil, vinegar, lemon zest and lemon juice and season to taste.

Put the sunflower seeds and pine nuts in a dry frying pan and toast over medium heat, tossing occasionally, for 2 minutes or until golden.

As soon as you drain the barley, tip it into a large bowl and mix in the dressing. Leave to cool for a few minutes, then mix in the sunflower seeds, pine nuts and dill. Top with the roasted beetroot (even better if it's still warm) and yoghurt, and season to taste.

SERVES 6

PIEDMONTESE CAPSICUMS

These capsicum boats appear on antipasto plates all over Italy. They're best eaten at room temperature, which makes them perfect for picnics. I pack them on a bed of salad leaves and by the time we've arrived, the capsicum's juices have made a lovely dressing: win–win. They're also a brilliant make-ahead side dish for barbecues. If you have any leftovers, they make a delicious pasta sauce when chopped finely and tossed about in a hot frying pan for 5 minutes.

4 red capsicums (peppers), halved and seeded
4 tomatoes, halved lengthways
8 anchovy fillets, drained and finely chopped
4 garlic cloves, finely chopped
2 Tbsp capers, rinsed and chopped
2 Tbsp olive oil
1 Tbsp balsamic vinegar
Mixed salad leaves, to serve
1 handful basil leaves

Preheat the oven to 180°C (350°F). Lightly oil a large ovenproof dish. Add the capsicum halves, cut side up and well spaced, then place a tomato half, cut side up, inside each capsicum half.

Combine the anchovies, garlic and capers. Scatter over the tomato halves, then drizzle with the oil and vinegar. Bake for 45 minutes or until the capsicums and tomatoes are soft and tender.

Put the salad leaves and basil on a platter and top with the capsicums and all their beautiful juices.

SERVES 6–8

Both of these are great at
room temperature, making them
perfect to take on a picnic.

WHOLEMEAL APPLE AND MARMALADE CAKE
(AKA THE GOOD, STURDY PICNIC CAKE)

If this cake were a woman, she'd wear sensible shoes. She'd be a reliable, fun, and self-deprecating sort of Chummy/Miranda Hart character. She wouldn't mind if you burnt her bottom, and she'd be a good sport about being transported over rough paddocks for a picnic and maybe even dropped, in which case she'd mostly hold her shape and taste great, even if she looked like a mess. She can also take any fruit you throw at her (within reason), plus she lasts for ages and is easy to make.

1 cup (100 g) almond meal (using freshly roasted, ground almonds makes a big difference)

1¼ cups (185 g) wholemeal plain flour

2 tsp baking powder

½ tsp ground cinnamon

½ tsp ground allspice

A pinch of salt

200 g (7 oz) butter, softened

¾ cup (165 g) firmly packed soft brown sugar

3 eggs, at room temperature

3 apples, cut into small chunks (I don't bother peeling them, but go ahead if you prefer)

½ cup (75 g) dried currants or raisins

¾ cup (250 g) marmalade

¼ cup (50 g) demerara sugar

Preheat the oven to 160°C (320°F). Grease a 23–24 cm (9–9½ inch) spring-form cake tin and line with baking paper.

Combine the almond meal, flour, baking powder, spices and salt in a bowl and whisk to combine and get rid of any lumps.

In the bowl of an electric mixer with a paddle attachment, cream the butter and brown sugar together for 5 minutes or until pale and fluffy. Add the eggs, one at a time, beating well after each addition. Fold in the flour mixture, then stir in the apple chunks and currants or raisins. Fold in the marmalade.

Transfer the batter to the tin, smooth the top and sprinkle with the demerara sugar. Bake for 1 hour or until the cake is just pulling away from the side of the tin and feels slightly firm to the touch. Leave to cool in the tin.

NOTE
Do wait until the cake has cooled down before moving it around too much. Any cake fresh out of the oven is going to crumble or crack if you try to get it out of the tin while still warm.

SERVES 8

All this cake asks is to be served with a thermos of strong tea.

DARK CHOCOLATE, GINGER AND ALMOND CLUSTERS

These are so easy they're hardly a recipe, but so delicious you really should give them a go. A great dessert for picnics (keep them in a cool box or chiller bag, though) and dinner parties when you can't stand plating up another course and all that extra washing up. Just pop them on a plate with a little fresh fruit and maybe some nougat or Turkish delight. I think that's all people want after a big meal – something sweet to nibble on with their last glass of wine (or two). They're also really yummy with a sprinkle of Sweet dukkah (page 75).

1 cup (150 g) chopped best-quality dark chocolate
1 cup (125 g) slivered almonds, toasted
1/2 cup (95 g) stem ginger, roughly chopped

Line a baking tray with baking paper.

Melt the chocolate in a glass bowl over a saucepan of simmering water (or however you prefer to melt chocolate). Once melted, let the chocolate cool a little, then stir in the almonds and ginger.

Scoop a tablespoon of the chocolate mixture onto the tray, keeping it in a nice round mound. Repeat with the remaining mixture. Pop in the fridge for at least an hour before serving.

NOTE
Variations to this recipe are endless, but here are a couple of ideas: swap the slivered almonds with hazelnuts and the ginger with dried figs; or swap the almonds with pistachios and the ginger with chopped Turkish delight.

MAKES ABOUT 15

SALTED PEANUT AND WHITE CHOCOLATE COOKIES

Here's one for the salty/sweet lovers. These are a gorgeous combination of salty peanuts and creamy white chocolate bound up in a crunchy, buttery biscuit, perfect with a morning coffee and also excellent crumbled over vanilla ice cream. One of the wonderful people who tested recipes for this book, the lovely Viktorija from Lithuania, said she made these without the caster sugar and they were the perfect sweetness for her taste. Feel free to do the same if your sweet tooth isn't perhaps as bad as my family's.

1 cup (150 g) plain flour
1/2 tsp baking powder
125 g (4 1/2 oz) unsalted butter, softened
1/2 cup (140 g) peanut butter
1/2 cup (110 g) firmly packed soft brown sugar
1/4 cup (55 g) caster sugar
1 egg
1 tsp natural vanilla extract
1/2 cup (80 g) salted peanuts
1 cup (140 g) white chocolate pieces
Vanilla salt (page 74) or regular sea salt,
* for sprinkling*

Preheat the oven to 180°C (350°F). Line two baking trays with baking paper.

Sift together the flour and baking powder and set aside. Cream the butter, peanut butter and sugars together until pale and fluffy. Add the egg and vanilla and beat to combine. Fold in the peanuts and white chocolate, then fold in the flour and baking powder.

Roll a walnut-sized piece of dough into a ball and place on a tray. Repeat with the remaining mixture. Use the tines of a fork to gently press each ball down, then sprinkle with the vanilla salt or regular sea salt.

Bake the cookies for 10–12 minutes or until golden brown. Let them cool on a wire rack, then transfer to an airtight container.

MAKES ABOUT 12–16

Happy campers

Simple chicken and chorizo paella ~ Bircher muesli ~ Wholemeal pancakes
Salted caramel sauce for everything ~ Tom's chocolate cake

My love of camping blossomed only recently, around the time we took ownership of a 1970s pop-up trailer that we all adore. It features a proper double mattress, a little annexe for a couple of swags and a basic outdoor kitchen, and it's by far and away the least slick set up in any camping ground.

Even though there's quite a bit of preparation involved in getting packed up and on the road (both at the beginning and end of any camping trip), there's also nothing quite like that first beer or glass of bubbles sitting around an open fire. Our camping food is fairly simple but tasty and generally well received, so I go with the old 'if it ain't broke…' theory. Lunch is generally wraps or sandwiches and dinner is a big paella, but it's camping breakfast where I really get carried away. And we always take a big slab of Tom's chocolate cake for morning tea or after lunch.

My love of camping blossomed
when we took ownership of a
1970s pop-up trailer.

SIMPLE CHICKEN AND CHORIZO PAELLA

I fall back on this recipe every time I go to make paella because it's always such a hit. Kids love it, teenagers inhale it and it makes adults happy too. Plus, if you have a nice big pan, this is an excellent and easy way to feed a large group. You can, of course, halve or even quarter the quantities below and cook it in a frying pan on the stove – hardly authentic, but neither is the recipe. Any leftovers can be formed into patties and fried as little rice cakes.

When I'm making this dish for camping or a picnic, I prepare the stock before we leave and keep it hot in a big thermos, ready to pour in when the time's right.

3 x 400 g (14 oz) tins whole peeled
  tomatoes
1/3 cup (90 g) tomato paste
  (concentrated purée)
1/4 cup (25 g) smoked paprika
1 tsp sea salt and a good grinding
  of fresh black pepper
1/4 cup (10 g) finely chopped
  rosemary
1/4 cup (10 g) finely chopped sage
A good pinch of saffron threads
  (or more if funds allow!)
8 cups (2 litres) chicken stock
1/4 cup (60 ml) olive oil
4 chorizo sausages, cut into 1 cm
  (1/2 inch) discs
5 garlic cloves, squashed with the
  flat side of a knife
800 g (1 lb 12 oz) skinless chicken
  thigh fillets, cut into 3 cm
  (1 1/4 inch) cubes
1 kg (2 lb 4 oz) calasparra rice
  (or at a pinch, any risotto rice)
2 cups (280 g) frozen peas
A couple of handfuls of roughly
  chopped flat-leaf parsley
3 lemons, quartered
1 baguette, sliced
Sliced fresh chilli or chilli flakes,
  to serve (optional)

Start by making the stock – this is where the flavour really comes from and by making it in advance, you cut out a fair few steps when it comes to paella time. In a large saucepan, combine the tomatoes, tomato paste, paprika, salt and pepper, herbs, saffron and chicken stock. Stir well and bring to the boil, then reduce the heat and simmer for a good 30 minutes. Check for seasoning – the stock should be richly flavoured and aromatic.

When ready to cook, place a paella pan over high heat and add the olive oil. Cook the chorizo, garlic and chicken for about 5 minutes, until the chicken is browned on the edges but only half cooked. Add the rice and stir for a couple of minutes. Pour in the tomato stock, reduce the heat to medium–low and leave to cook for about 10 minutes, without stirring. Top up the liquid with water if necessary and check the rice. If it's still crunchy, keep cooking and top up with a little more water if it looks like it's drying out. Try not to stir it much because you want a nice 'crust' to develop on the bottom of the pan. The rice should be tender with just the slightest crunch. Once it reaches that point, add the peas and a little more water if necessary (you don't want the paella to be dry at all). Cook for a few more minutes or until the peas are bright green.

Serve the hot paella with the parsley, a bunch of lemon wedges and the sliced baguette. I also put a dish of chilli on the side for the heat seekers.

SERVES 12–14

BIRCHER MUESLI

This is the best possible camping breakfast – it's all portioned up and ready to eat, and it's completely delicious and filling.

1 granny smith apple (unpeeled), grated
1 1/2 cups (150 g) rolled oats
1/4 cup (50 g) chia seeds
1/2 cup (125 ml) apple juice
1 cup (260 g) plain yoghurt
A pinch of ground cinnamon
Poached apricots (page 74), to serve

Mix the grated apple, oats, chia seeds, apple juice, yoghurt and cinnamon together. Divide among jars, cover and place in the fridge overnight.

Serve the muesli with the poached apricots or your choice of toppings.

TOPPING IDEAS
~ extra yoghurt or milk
~ fresh berries or other fruit
~ poached apples or quinces
~ Rhubarb compote (page 74)
~ toasted and roughly chopped nuts
~ Sweet dukkah (page 75)
~ a sprinkling of brown sugar
~ a drizzle of honey or maple syrup

SERVES 4

WHOLEMEAL PANCAKES

These pancakes are a big hit whether camping or at home. If you are considering the former, I suggest you make up the batter back at the ranch, then transfer it to a large plastic piping bag and seal the ends. Store it in the cool box or chiller bag and then, when it's breakfast time, just snip off the end and pipe straight into a hot, buttered frying pan.

1 cup (150 g) wholemeal plain flour
2 tsp baking powder
1 cup (250 ml) milk
1 egg
Grated zest of 1 orange
2 Tbsp caster sugar
Butter, for cooking

Combine all the ingredients in a small bowl and whisk until well combined. Store in the fridge until needed.

When ready to cook the pancakes, melt a knob of butter in a frying pan over medium heat. Cook a few tablespoons of batter at a time, cooking for a minute or so on each side. Flip once bubbles appear on the surface of the pancakes.

Serve the pancakes with poached fruit (pictured here is the Rhubarb compote from page 74), fresh fruit, caramel sauce, maple syrup and bacon or the classic lemon and sugar.

SERVES 6–8

Carry the pancake batter in a piping bag, then snip off the end and pipe straight into the frying pan.

SALTED CARAMEL SAUCE FOR EVERYTHING

This is one for my dad, who is absolutely mad for a good caramel sauce. The last time we went camping I packed a jar of this and we had it on pancakes, shaken up in a jar full of ice and milk (plus a shot of cold-brewed coffee for Tim and me), and poured over ice cream. It lasts for ages and makes a great gift. And it tastes amazing. If you're serving it as a topping, consider finishing off with a sprinkle of Vanilla salt (page 74).

You'll find the sauce thickens up quite a lot in the fridge. To soften it, either place the jar in a bowl of hot water, give it a quick zap in the microwave or transfer it to a saucepan and gently warm the sauce until it loosens up.

1¾ cups (390 g) caster sugar
170 g (5¾ oz) unsalted butter, cut into cubes
1 cup (250 ml) single (pure) cream
Seeds from 1 vanilla bean
1 tsp sea salt

Put the sugar in a saucepan over medium–high heat and cook, stirring often, until it melts into a smooth caramel (watch it carefully towards the end because it can go from perfectly golden to burnt in the blink of an eye). As soon as the sugar is completely melted and smooth, add the butter and whisk until it has melted into a smooth sauce.

Remove the pan from the heat. Whisk in the cream, vanilla seeds and salt. Return to the heat and bring to the boil. Cook, stirring often, for 5 minutes, then remove from the heat and divide among jars. Store in the fridge for up to a month.

MAKES ABOUT 2 CUPS

TOM'S CHOCOLATE CAKE

This cake is my son Tom's all-time favourite and he's not alone – I've found kids love this for its mellow flavour and soft, springy texture. I love it because it takes all of 5 minutes to throw together. Super simple. Super easy. I always take this cake camping, to picnics, sports days, etc., and it disappears in seconds.

1½ cups (225 g) self-raising flour
¼ cup (30 g) cocoa powder
1¼ cups (275 g) caster sugar
3 eggs, at room temperature
125 g (4½ oz) butter, softened and cut into cubes
½ cup (125 ml) milk
1 tsp vanilla bean paste

Chocolate icing
1 cup (160 g) icing sugar
2 Tbsp cocoa powder
50 g (1¾ oz) butter, softened
2 Tbsp milk
Sprinkles, to decorate

Preheat the oven to 180°C (350°F). Grease and line a 20 cm (8 inch) square cake tin with baking paper.

Combine all the ingredients in the bowl of an electric mixer and beat for 5 minutes. Spoon into the cake tin and bake for 30 minutes or until a skewer comes out clean. Let the cake cool in the tin for about 5 minutes before turning out to cool completely on a wire rack.

For the icing, sift the icing sugar and cocoa into a small bowl. Add the butter and milk and whisk until smooth (or use an electric mixer). Spread the icing over the cake and top with the sprinkles.

VARIATION
Leave out the cocoa (make up the weight in extra flour) and instead add the grated zest of a lemon or a generous teaspoon of mixed spice.

SERVES 6–8

Set up an outdoor kitchen and bring together some friends for a day of preserving.

Autumn preserving

Apple butter ~ Buttermilk scones ~ Quince butter
Erika's cabbage and caraway kraut ~ Roasted tomato passata

Autumn is the most generous of seasons – from pomme fruits in the orchard (apples, pears and quinces), to gluts of tomatoes in the garden and the end of summer's berries, figs and plums. So it follows that this is the time of year to set aside a day or so, bring together some friends and put away this goodness for the leaner winter and early spring months.

I know that preserving and pickling and bottling can be a messy business, especially if, like me, you have a small house and kitchen that gets very hot and sticky very quickly. Here's a tip I've adopted recently from a friend: head to your local camping shop and buy a cheap gas burner ring, then set up a trestle in the garden and do all your chopping, cooking and preserving outdoors. You know how they say that food tastes better outside? Well, I think food is also more fun to make outside, especially when preserving.

APPLE BUTTER

If you haven't tried apple butter, I recommend you give it a try. It's absolutely delicious and when you make it your kitchen smells amazing and you can almost imagine you are Diane Keaton in *Baby Boom*. All that will be missing is Sam Shepard walking through the door with that smile.

Apple butter is gorgeous with scones, on pancakes, sandwiched with cream between a sponge cake, over toast or even whizzed up with ice-cold milk for an apple shake. I particularly like it with a dollop of whipped cream and buttermilk scones.

8 large cooking apples (I use granny smith apples)
2 tsp lemon juice
2 Tbsp caster sugar
1/2 tsp ground cinnamon

Peel, core and quarter the apples, then place in an ovenproof saucepan. Add 1/2 cup (125 ml) water, the lemon juice, sugar and cinnamon. Cook over medium heat, stirring every now and then, for 30 minutes or until the apples have collapsed into a soft mush.

Preheat the oven to 150°C (300°F).

Transfer the apple mixture to a food processor and blitz until smooth. Return to the pan and cover with a lid or foil. Place in the oven for 1 hour, stirring halfway through to make sure the mixture doesn't catch on the bottom. Transfer the apple butter to jars and seal. Keep in the fridge for up to a month.

MAKES ABOUT 2 CUPS

BUTTERMILK SCONES

These buttermilk scones are rather rich and beautifully fluffy. They're absolutely delicious with the classic jam and cream combo, but especially good with a little quince or apple butter and perhaps a dollop of crème fraîche or yoghurt to cut through the richness.

2³/4 cups (410 g) plain flour, plus extra for dusting
1/2 cup (110 g) caster sugar, plus extra for sprinkling
1/2 cup (100 g) soft brown sugar
2 Tbsp baking powder
1 tsp bicarbonate of soda
A good pinch of sea salt
125 g (4¹/2 oz) unsalted butter, cubed
1 cup (250 ml) buttermilk
1 egg
1/4 cup (60 ml) single (pure) cream

Combine the flour, caster sugar, brown sugar, baking powder, bicarbonate of soda and salt in the bowl of a food processor. Add the butter and blitz until the mixture just resembles coarse breadcrumbs. Pour in the buttermilk and blitz again for just a second, so that everything is barely combined.

Turn the mixture out onto a lightly floured surface and, working quickly, bring it together into a dough. Press the dough out until it's about 2 cm (³/4 inch) thick. Use a 6 cm (2¹/2 inch) cutter or sharp knife to cut the dough into rounds or triangles. Place on a baking tray lined with baking paper, then cover and place in the freezer for at least an hour.

Preheat the oven to 180°C (350°F). Whisk the egg and cream together to make an egg wash. Generously brush the scones with the egg wash and sprinkle with caster sugar, then cook in the oven for 20 minutes or until golden.

MAKES 8–10

QUINCE BUTTER

Quinces are my favourite fruit. Every autumn, I pick and poach every last one not only from the tree in our orchard but also the wild quince tree that grows in a paddock nearby. I horrify my children by jumping a fence to get to this tree every April. For years I'd drive past and watch the birds eat every last quince, so now I indulge in a little light trespassing and pick a basket, and the sky hasn't fallen in yet.

The idea of a quince butter is simple: peel, chop, poach or stew the fruit, then purée and roast in the oven to thicken up. The result is a smooth, brightly coloured and intensely flavoured butter-free butter. Use it wherever you'd reach for lemon curd or similar. I think it's amazing spread on sourdough toast with mellow, creamy ricotta, but I also enjoy it on top of yoghurt, or stir it through a vanilla custard and then freeze it for quince ice cream.

The extra nice thing about making a batch of quince butter is that when you give it away, people get super excited. I think that's probably because they've never had it before, the colour and flavour are insanely good, and they can feel the love you put into making it.

4–6 quinces
2 cups (440 g) sugar
Juice of 1 lemon
1 Tbsp vanilla bean paste
1 cinnamon stick

First you need to poach the quinces. Start by preheating the oven to 150°C (300°F).

Peel, core and quarter the quinces, reserving the cores.

Combine the sugar, lemon juice, vanilla bean paste and cinnamon in a saucepan and bring to the boil. Stir over medium heat until the sugar has dissolved, then simmer for a few minutes.

Meanwhile, arrange the quince pieces in a deep roasting tin in a single layer. Don't worry if they colour a little – this won't affect the end result. Tie the cores together in a piece of muslin and add it to the tin (I never seem to have any muslin on hand, so I just scatter a few cores over the top of the quinces then fish them out later). The cores will add colour and pectin to the fruit while cooking.

Pour the sugar syrup over the quinces and cover tightly with foil. Place in the oven for 3–4 hours or until the quinces have turned a ruby-red colour and are deliciously aromatic. Remove and discard the cores and cinnamon stick.

Let the quinces cool a little, then tip them into a food processor, syrup and all, and blitz until really smooth. Pour the puréed quince back into the roasting tin and return (uncovered) to the oven for 1 hour. This will really thicken things up nicely and intensify the flavour, too. Stir every 20 minutes to make sure the bottom doesn't burn, then transfer the quince butter to jars and seal. Keep in the fridge for up to a month.

MAKES ABOUT 2 CUPS

ERIKA'S CABBAGE AND CARAWAY KRAUT

Erika Watson of Epicurean Harvest is a friend and regular guest at my workshops. With partner Hayden Druce, she grows superb produce on their small plot in the Blue Mountains. She has a wealth of knowledge on preserving and storing seasonal excess, and this is her recipe.

Kraut is one of the simplest fermented foods around – basically cabbage leaves and salt become kraut through the process of lactic acid fermentation. By massaging the cabbage with salt, the beneficial bacteria on the surface converts sugars in the cabbage into lactic acid. This, in turn, halts the growth of harmful bacteria and creates a delicious cocktail of vitamins, enzymes and super-friendly bacteria, all of which are great for the digestive system.

If you are new to the world of fermented foods, kraut is a great place to start. It's a simple process for which you need no special equipment – just a big jar, salt and a little time. If you have a friend who has been unwell, taking rounds of antibiotics and such, a jar of kraut will be a welcome present, not only delicious but so healthy, too.

1 large savoy cabbage
3 tsp salt
1 Tbsp caraway seeds

THINGS TO DO WITH KRAUT

~ Start with the classic – pile atop a sandwich of rye bread with pastrami.
~ Dollop a tablespoon or so on top of a winter minestrone to add tang and crunch.
~ Use it as a bed for a nice fried or softly poached egg – break the egg into the kraut and stir it through, then serve with toasted sourdough.
~ Bake a potato or sweet potato in its skin, then cut open and pile in sour cream and kraut. A super-filling, yummy and healthy lunch or dinner.
~ Make up a big bowl of brown rice, veggies, nuts and maybe a fried egg, then finish with a good dollop of kraut.

Remove about five or six outer leaves from the cabbage and set aside for later. Using a large sharp knife, finely chop the whole cabbage, removing the core. Measure 13 cups (1 kg) chopped cabbage into a large bowl and add the salt and caraway seeds.

Either with a heavy pestle or your fists, pound, grab, squeeze and rub the cabbage until it's covered by its own juices that are produced by all that pounding and squeezing. Set aside for 10 minutes for the cabbage to soften, then bash and squeeze again for a few more minutes. The aim is to create enough juices to cover the cabbage once it's packed. At this point, transfer the cabbage to a wide-mouthed jar (wide enough for your fist to fit through). Push the pounded cabbage really firmly to the bottom of the jar so that the juices sit about 2.5 cm (1 inch) over the surface of the cabbage. (I use the pestle from my mortar and pestle.)

Take the reserved cabbage leaves and push them down on top of the cabbage, so they are also sitting under the liquid, acting as 'leaf seals'. Place a weight on top of the leaves, push down and seal with a lid. (I use a jar filled with water, which fits through the big jar's opening.)

Leave the cabbage to stand out of direct sunlight or covered with a tea towel for 10–14 days, depending on the time of year (in warmer weather, the fermentation process usually takes about 10 days, but it takes longer in colder weather).

Remove the weight, pour off the liquid and discard the cabbage leaf seals. (Sometimes these leaves become infected with airborne fungi or bacteria, but don't worry – they're there to protect the kraut below.) Fork the kraut into smaller jars and store in the fridge.

MAKES 1 BIG JAR

ROASTED TOMATO PASSATA

This passata is a simple enough recipe but it produces a sauce of such deep flavour that I hope you'll make it often. Roasting your tomatoes and then puréeing and bottling them is the easiest and arguably the best way to preserve seasonal gluts of this glorious fruit (no peeling, no fiddling). Even better, gather a few friends on an autumn morning and get everyone to bring one thing: a box of tomatoes, all the jars, the garlic and oil, and set aside a few hours to chop, roast, chat, bottle and drink tea.

5 kg (11 lb) vine-ripened tomatoes, cut into chunks
6 brown onions, cut into eighths
1 garlic bulb, cloves separated
1/4 cup (60 ml) olive oil
1 tsp sea salt
1/2 tsp chilli flakes

Preheat the oven to 180°C (350°F). Divide all the ingredients among a few big roasting tins and toss to combine. Roast for 45 minutes or until the tomatoes and onions are completely softened and cooked through.

Remove the garlic and squeeze the roasted pulp into the roasting tins. Transfer the mixture in batches to a blender or food processor and blitz to a smooth sauce. Pour into sterilised bottles or jars and seal tightly.

You can store the bottles of passata in the fridge for up to a month, or heat preserve them so they last you right through winter. If you have a Fowlers preserving unit, follow the instructions that came with it. If you're using a stockpot, line the base with a folded tea towel, place the bottles on top and tuck a few tea towels between them so they don't clink together and break when the water boils. Bring to the boil, then reduce the heat a little and cook for 1 hour (you may need to top up the water every now and then).

Carefully remove the bottles from the preserving unit or pot and wipe down. Store in a cool dark place.

MAKES ABOUT 4 LITRES (140 FL OZ)

IDEAS FOR USING TOMATO PASSATA

~ Give away a bottle with a nice packet of pasta and a hunk of cheese.
~ Use it as a pizza sauce.
~ Pour over meatballs, chicken thigh pieces or cannelloni stuffed with ricotta and spinach, and bake.
~ Thin out with a good stock, season with salt and pepper and serve as a super-tasty tomato soup.
~ Add to a winter minestrone for some bright summer flavour.

FRESH ALMOND MILK

1 cup (160 g) raw almonds
A pinch of sea salt
2 pitted dates

Soak the almonds overnight in cold water. Drain and tip into a high-powered blender along with the salt and 1 cup (250 ml) water and blitz for 30 seconds or until you have a smooth paste. Add the dates and 2 cups (500 ml) water and blitz for 1 minute. Grab a piece of muslin (or a nut milk bag) and drape it over a large sieve. Pour the almond milk through the sieve and squeeze out as much liquid as possible. Store the milk in the fridge for a couple of days. Give it a shake before using. You can use the left-over pulp in muesli or bread dough, or feed it to your chooks like I do.

MAKES ABOUT 3 CUPS

HOME-MADE CRÈME FRAÎCHE

1 cup (250 ml) single (pure) cream
2 Tbsp buttermilk

Whisk the cream and buttermilk in a large jar. Place a layer of muslin or a clean Chux cloth on top and secure with twine or an elastic band, to stop bugs, dust or anything else getting into the mixture.

Leave the mixture to do its thing on the bench for 24 hours – it should thicken to the consistency of a good Greek-style yoghurt. If needed, leave it for another 24 hours. Stir well, transfer to a container with a lid and store in the fridge for up to 2 weeks.

MAKES ABOUT 1 CUP

VANILLA SALT

1 cup (225 g) sea salt flakes
2 vanilla beans, split lengthways

Place the sea salt in a small bowl. Scrape the vanilla seeds into the salt, and use your fingers to work them together. Divide the vanilla salt into small jars and add the empty vanilla beans (they'll keep imparting flavour). Serve with ripe tomatoes or poached fruit.

MAKES ABOUT 1 CUP

POACHED APRICOTS

1/2 cup (110 g) caster sugar
1/2 cup (125 ml) wine
1 tsp vanilla bean paste
1 kg (2 lb 4 oz) apricots, halved, stones removed

Combine the sugar, wine and vanilla in a large saucepan and bring to the boil. Add the apricots, then reduce the heat to a low simmer and cover the mixture with a piece of baking paper. Cook for 5 minutes or until the apricots are soft, then remove from the heat. Store in the fridge.

MAKES ABOUT 2 CUPS

RHUBARB COMPOTE

1 bunch (300 g/10 1/2 oz) rhubarb, trimmed
1 vanilla bean, split lengthways
Juice of 2 oranges
1/3 cup (75 g) caster sugar

Preheat the oven to 180°C (350°F). Line a small roasting tin with baking paper. Cut the rhubarb into 3 cm (1 1/4 inch) batons and add to the tin with the vanilla bean, orange juice and sugar. Toss well, then cover with foil and roast for 25 minutes or until the rhubarb has completely collapsed.

MAKES ABOUT 2 CUPS

GROUND TOASTED CARDAMOM

¹/₃ cup (35 g) cardamom pods

Preheat the oven to 140°C (275°F). Scatter the cardamom pods over a baking tray and bake for 10 minutes or until beginning to turn dark green. Cool, then transfer to a high-powered blender, food processor, spice grinder or coffee grinder and blitz as finely as possible. Pass through a sieve to remove any larger pieces.

Store in an airtight container as the best ground cardamom ever.

MAKES ABOUT 1¹/₂ TABLESPOONS

SWEET DUKKAH

¹/₂ cup (75 g) hazelnuts or walnuts
¹/₃ cup (50 g) sesame seeds
2 Tbsp poppy seeds
¹/₂ tsp coriander seeds
²/₃ cup (100 g) raw unsalted pistachio nuts
¹/₂ tsp ground toasted cardamom (see above)
¹/₂ tsp ground cinnamon
¹/₄ tsp ground nutmeg
2 Tbsp soft brown sugar
A pinch of sea salt

Preheat the oven to 180°C (350°F). Spread the hazelnuts or walnuts on a baking tray and toast for 5 minutes. Add the sesame seeds, poppy seeds and coriander seeds and continue to toast for another 5 minutes. Remove from the oven.

Combine the hazelnuts or walnuts and pistachios in a food processor or use a mortar and pestle and blitz or bash until the mixture resembles coarse breadcrumbs. Add the toasted seeds, spices, brown sugar and salt. Give it another quick blitz or bash and mix to combine, then store in a jar or airtight container.

MAKES ABOUT 1¹/₂ CUPS

LEMON AND PASSIONFRUIT CURD

220 g (7³/₄ oz) unsalted butter
1²/₃ cups (370 g) caster sugar
Grated zest and juice of 4 lemons – you need ³/₄ cup (185 ml) juice
6 eggs, lightly beaten
¹/₂ cup (125 g) passionfruit pulp (you'll need about 4 passionfruit)

Put the butter, sugar and lemon zest in a glass bowl resting over a saucepan of simmering water. Cook, stirring often, for about 5 minutes until the butter has melted and the sugar has dissolved.

Add the eggs, lemon juice and passionfruit pulp and cook, gently whisking, for 20 minutes or until the mixture has thickened and coats the back of a wooden spoon – if you have a sugar thermometer, setting point will be around 80°C (176°F). Spoon into clean jars, seal and keep in the fridge for up to 2 weeks.

NOTE
If you prefer to make just lemon curd, leave out the passionfruit and add one more lemon.

MAKES ABOUT 5 CUPS

ACKNOWLEDGEMENTS

This book is for Tim, Alice and Tom. Our little family is everything to me. Thank you, guys, for your love and support, and, right back at you.

As anyone whose primary income depends on primary industry knows, the farming life can be really hard. It's a juggle, a gamble and a 24 hour/ 7 days a week job. And yes, it's a cliche, but despite the challenges we do look around us every day and feel grateful we get to live here on this farm, in this place together. Thank you, Tim and ALL of the farmers who grow and produce our food, for keeping the boat afloat through drought, bushfires, all the uncertainties and challenges.

Thank you to my parents, Annie and Henry Herron, whose beautiful property features prominently throughout this book. Thank you for giving my siblings and me confidence, opportunity and a home we always love to come back to.

Thank you to the team at Murdoch Books, especially Corinne Roberts who has guided me through this process with such skill and warmth, and designer Vivien Valk who has worked so hard to make this book so beautiful.

Big thanks to Josie Chapman for opening up her beautiful cottages at the Old Convent B&B Borenore for some of the photography.

Making and sharing good, simple, seasonal food is an act of love and generosity, so my final thanks is to you, for buying this book and hopefully taking inspiration from it to go out and leave a basket of home-made food at someone's door soon. It will mean so much to them.

This edition published in 2020 by Murdoch Books, an imprint of Allen & Unwin
Content originally published in *A Basket by the Door*, published in 2019 by Murdoch Books

Murdoch Books UK
Ormond House, 26–27 Boswell Street,
London, WC1N 3JZ
Phone: +44 (0) 20 8785 5995
murdochbooks.co.uk
info@murdochbooks.co.uk

For corporate orders & custom publishing contact our business development team at salesenquiries@murdochbooks.com.au

Publisher: Corinne Roberts
Cover design: northwoodgreen.com
Internal design: Vivien Valk
Editor: Justine Harding
Production director: Lou Playfair

Photography: Sophie Hansen, except page 2 by Clancy Paine

ISBN 978 1 911 63281 8

A catalogue record for this book is available from the British Library

Printed by C&C Offset Printing Co Ltd, China

TABLESPOONS: We have used Australian 20 ml (4 teaspoon) tablespoon measures. If you are using a smaller European 15 ml (3 teaspoon) tablespoon, add an extra teaspoon of the ingredient for each tablespoon specified in the recipe.

10 9 8 7 6 5 4 3 2 1